# THE
# Hopeful
# NEIGHBORHOOD

## FIELD GUIDE

Six Sessions on Pursuing the
Common Good Right Where You Live

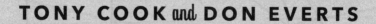

## TONY COOK and DON EVERTS

An imprint of InterVarsity Press
Downers Grove, Illinois

InterVarsity Press
P.O. Box 1400, Downers Grove, IL 60515-1426
ivpress.com
email@ivpress.com

InterVarsity Press® is the book-publishing division of InterVarsity Christian Fellowship/USA®, a movement of students and faculty active on campus at hundreds of universities, colleges, and schools of nursing in the United States of America, and a member movement of the International Fellowship of Evangelical Students. For information about local and regional activities, visit intervarsity.org.

Scripture quotations, unless otherwise noted, are from The Holy Bible, English Standard Version, copyright © 2001 by Crossway Bibles, a division of Good News Publishers. Used by permission. All rights reserved.

While any stories in this book are true, some names and identifying information may have been changed to protect the privacy of individuals.

All figures designed by Sarah Eischer, copyright Lutheran Hour Ministries.

The publisher cannot verify the accuracy or functionality of website URLs used in this book beyond the date of publication.

Cover design and image composite: Cindy Kiple
Interior design: Jeanna Wiggins
Images: compass and map: © nicoolay / E+ / Getty Images
        compass: © bortonia / DigitalVision Vectors / Getty Images
        gated community illustration: © Imagezoo / Getty Images

ISBN 978-0-8308-4732-7 (print)
ISBN 978-0-8308-4733-4 (digital)

Printed in the United States of America ♾

InterVarsity Press is committed to ecological stewardship and to the conservation of natural resources in all our operations. This book was printed using sustainably sourced paper.

**Library of Congress Cataloging-in-Publication Data**
A catalog record for this book is available from the Library of Congress.

| P | 24 | 23 | 22 | 21 | 20 | 19 | 18 | 17 | 16 | 15 | 14 | 13 | 12 | 11 | 10 | 9 | 8 | 7 | 6 | 5 | 4 | 3 | 2 | 1 |
|---|----|----|----|----|----|----|----|----|----|----|----|----|----|----|----|---|---|---|---|---|---|---|---|---|
| Y | 41 | 40 | 39 | 38 | 37 | 36 | 35 | 34 | 33 | 32 | 31 | 30 | 29 | 28 | 27 | 26 | 25 | 24 | 23 | 22 | 21 |

**Dedicated**

*to all those who still believe*

*they can make a difference*

*right where they live.*

# Contents

# Introduction

## YOU AND YOUR NEIGHBORHOOD

*The people who live in a particular locale
are the experts on that place.*

JAY WALLJASPER

We believe real change and hope begin with the real experts of a neighborhood: those who actually live in that neighborhood. We believe *you* are an expert on your own neighborhood, and we believe you are surrounded by other experts. And that's why we've written this field guide: to inspire and equip people just like you to pursue the common good in your own neighborhood.

You see, we are convinced that everyone has gifts to share and everyone is created to pursue the common good of their neighborhood. It's these two convictions that have made us excited about what we call "hopeful neighborhoods."

> **HOPEFUL NEIGHBORHOOD:** "a neighborhood where people work together to pursue neighborhood well-being as the highest form of common good."

Based on the fact that you have picked up this field guide and are reading this introduction, we assume we have something in common with you: we live somewhere and have taken more than a passing interest in that place.

The two of us happen to live in the St. Louis area, but we haven't always lived here. Tony has lived in twenty different neighborhoods in both the United States and Australia during his life, and Don has lived in thirty different neighborhoods. But we are both interested in where we live right now.

**NEIGHBORHOOD:** "a geographically localized area characterized by a shared sense of boundaries among its residents."

Tony lives in Lindenwood Park, an urban neighborhood featuring a mix of retail businesses and residential homes, some of which date back to the family farms of the late 1800s. Don lives in Pierremont, a suburban neighborhood with two public schools, four churches, one mosque, one Hindu temple, and both a Costco and a Walmart.

We are both neighbors within our neighborhoods and members of the larger community in which our neighborhoods sit. We care about our neighborhoods, and that is why we are writing a field guide about pursuing the common good right where you live.

**COMMUNITY:** "a geographically localized area characterized by a zip code."

We are neighbors. We are not experts in community development or urban planning or civic engagement—though we think long and hard about these topics. Pursuing the common good of a neighborhood is not our academic specialty—though we've read extensively about it. We are writing as neighbors who are part of a collaborative network committed to improving neighborhood well-being around the world: the Hopeful Neighborhood Project.

The Hopeful Neighborhood Project's resources and online network equip and encourage neighbors to work together, using their gifts and the gifts of their community, to pursue the common good of their neighborhood.

Our own passion for this project is fueled by our convictions as Christians, but the Hopeful Neighborhood Project includes neighbors of all faiths and creeds who want to pursue the common good right where they live. In the same way, this field guide is written for anyone who is interested in making a difference in their neighborhood. Together we will walk through six important lessons that are central to any efforts in your neighborhood.

But first we invite you to locate and name your own neighborhood. For some of you this may be easy, for others this may be a little tricky.

 **WELCOME TO MY NEIGHBORHOOD**
Go to www.hopefulneighborhood.org/fieldguide to see how Tony and Don located and named their own neighborhoods and learn how you can do the same.

The process of locating and naming your neighborhood is an important place to start. The lessons we are going through are not meant to be merely theoretical but are meant to be applied in your own neighborhood. So, where is your neighborhood?

Use figure 0.1 to draw a basic map of your community and neighborhood. What natural boundaries are there for each? What zip code do you live in? What is the name of your community? Does your neighborhood have a name?

# MAP MY NEIGHBORHOOD

## MY COMMUNITY
### ZIP CODE:

## MY NEIGHBORHOOD

**FIGURE 0.1. MY COMMUNITY AND NEIGHBORHOOD**

# Focus on Possibilities

## A HOPEFUL NEIGHBORHOOD IS WHERE POSSIBILITIES ARE THE FOCUS.

*Each community boasts a unique combination
of assets upon which to build its future.*

**JOHN L. McKNIGHT AND JOHN P. KRETZMANN**

N o matter what kind of neighborhood you live in—urban, suburban, rural, whatever—we are glad you've decided to invest time in thinking about it. We ourselves have found it fascinating and beneficial (and even life-changing) to be thoughtful about the people and place right where we live. And we are confident you will find the same to be true.

This is especially true if you are interested in pursuing the common good of your neighborhood. Many good things can come from even the simplest efforts to pursue the common good right where you live.

> **COMMON GOOD:** "the flourishing or wellbeing of the sum total of communal life in a given place."[1]

As you begin to think about this for your own neighborhood, it's important for you to consider how you will look at the people and place surrounding you.

In this session we invite you to learn about and contrast two very different ways of looking at your neighborhood: you can focus on problems or you can focus on possibilities. The difference between these two approaches is significant and the evidence is unambiguous: focusing on possibilities is what will foster a hopeful neighborhood.

Obviously, there are many aspects of your neighborhood you could focus on in order to pursue the common good. You could focus on something in your neighborhood that irritates you. Or you could identify a neighborhood initiative you've seen work somewhere else (like a neighborhood garden) and attempt to reproduce that initiative in your own neighborhood.

But in a hopeful neighborhood, *possibilities* are the focus.

When we talk about possibilities, we're talking about practical opportunities to pursue the common good that arise from the unique specifics of your neighborhood. These possibilities are ideas you might not think about if you were focusing on obvious problems or weaknesses.

> **POSSIBILITY:** "a specific path toward greater neighborhood well-being that relies on current gifts in the neighborhood."

Possibilities are powerful. They can liberate you from the tyranny of the urgent, help you avoid the small horizons of a problem mindset, and allow you to escape the trap of assuming that what worked in another neighborhood will work in yours.

Possibilities can show you an unexpected path right in your own neighborhood—a path that leads to a more hopeful horizon.

## WHAT'S YOUR FOCUS?

The power of focusing on possibilities rather than problems was first discussed by John L. McKnight and John P. Kretzmann. Their research in the early 1990s was based on various Chicago neighborhoods, and their findings challenged the traditional approach to neighborhood development.

**THE POWER OF FOCUSING ON POSSIBILITIES**
Go to www.hopefulneighborhood.org/fieldguide
to see for yourself how powerful it can be to
focus on possibilities rather than problems. Use
the space that follows to respond to the reflection
and discussion prompts in the video:

The traditional approach was to focus on what was wrong in a neighborhood: getting service providers and funding agencies to address needs and deficiencies. Kretzmann and McKnight's work illustrated how much stronger an asset-based approach is than this more familiar deficit-based approach.

**DEFICIT-BASED:** "a needs-driven approach to community in which solutions are sought for community problems."

**ASSET-BASED:** "a gifts-driven approach to community in which opportunities are sought for community possibilities."

Their 1993 book, *Building Communities from the Inside Out: A Path Toward Finding and Mobilizing a Community's Assets*, started a revolution in community development that caused leaders, nonprofits, and everyday neighbors to begin looking at neighborhoods with new eyes: focusing not on what was *wrong* in the neighborhood but on what was *strong* instead.

This refreshing, powerful approach (commonly referred to as "asset-based community development" or ABCD) involves developing a detailed "map" of all of the many assets, or gifts, within a neighborhood.

> **ASSET-BASED COMMUNITY DEVELOPMENT (ABCD):**
> "pursuing community or neighborhood revitalization by focusing on what is strong instead of what is wrong."

There are many advantages to this approach. As you consider pursuing the common good of your own neighborhood, it is important that you first consider some of the important distinctions between an asset-based and deficit-based approach.

>  **IMPLICATIONS OF FOCUSING ON ASSETS OR DEFICITS.** Go to www.hopefulneighborhood .org/fieldguide to understand the very practical implications of an asset-based and deficit-based approach to your neighborhood. Use the space below to respond to the reflection and discussion prompts in the video:

## FOCUSING ON POSSIBILITIES

When you start by focusing on what is strong rather than what is wrong in your own neighborhood, you will naturally begin to imagine possibilities. Possibilities are inherently about the future—a better future.

As you'll see in session three, there's something about mapping out your neighborhood's many assets, or gifts, that naturally suggests various hopeful possibilities for the future. These specific possibilities are what hope is all about. While focusing on what's wrong may or may not produce hope, focusing on what's *strong* produces hope naturally. This hope is based not on wishes alone but on the very real, very concrete possibilities that the gifts already in the neighborhood suggest.

## COMPARING APPROACHES

| Deficit-Based | Asset-Based |
|---|---|
| Wrong | Strong |
| Problems | Possibilities |
| What's Missing | What's There |
| Scarcity | Abundance |
| Needs | Assets |
| Outside-In Control | Inside-Out Leadership |
| Institution-Led | Neighbor-Led |
| Do To | Do With |
| Can't Do | Can Do |

FIGURE 1.1. TWO APPROACHES TO COMMUNITY DEVELOPMENT

In this way, focusing on possibilities takes you further than focusing on problems. And the experience of discovering gifts and the possibilities they naturally suggest is inherently hopeful for everyone in the neighborhood.

Don once had lunch with a member of the Hopeful Neighborhood Project who is committed to focusing on possibilities. As a simple thought experiment, Don and his friend pretended they lived on the same block and asked this question: *What are some neighborhood possibilities we can imagine based solely on the gifts the two of us have?*

Forty-five minutes later they were wide-eyed, genuinely excited about the possibilities, and wishing they really did live on the same block! Why? There's just something inherently hopeful and energizing about focusing on possibilities—even in a simple exercise like this.

So why don't more people begin by focusing on what's strong in their community or neighborhood? In short, because of unhealthy muscle memory.

## OUR KNEE-JERK PROBLEM MINDSET

*Muscle memory* is a term used to refer to an action you've done so many times that you now do it without thinking. Athletes strive for muscle memory. Baseball pitchers will throw a specific pitch over and over so that when they are in the game, they don't have to think about that pitch consciously—they can just throw it. For an athlete, muscle memory is a great thing.

But when you are taking your first steps in pursuing the common good of your neighborhood, muscle memory can be a problem. A problem mindset is so common that most of us have developed the knee-jerk habit of looking for difficulties. Without thinking, we default to focusing on what is wrong.

We may not have the fancy language for it, but most of us take a deficit-based approach to looking at our neighborhoods, whether we know we're doing it or not. In our work with the Hopeful

Neighborhood Project, we have seen this play out again and again: even people who are trying to focus on what's strong inevitably slip back into a problem mindset.

We once hosted a gathering of community development experts who are firm believers in an asset-based approach to neighborhood work. While together, we engaged in some possibility brainstorming exercises and were surprised by how often everyone there (including the two of us) defaulted to solving problems. This is how strong the knee-jerk focus on problems is within all of us.

This is why we all need to be encouraged from time to time to focus on what is strong in our neighborhood. And that is our encouragement to you.

## SESSION REVIEW

Begin your pursuit of the common good by taking some specific steps to conceptualize, personalize, and visualize what it would look like to intentionally focus on possibilities.

*Conceptualize.* Restate in your own words the advantages of an asset-based approach to looking at a neighborhood.

*Personalize.* Reflect on a specific time you personally saw or experienced a person or group using a deficit-based approach. How many of the deficit-based attributes listed in figure 1.1 did you see in action?

*Visualize.* Reflecting on that same experience, imagine how things might have gone differently with an asset-based approach.

## SUMMARY

We spent this session discovering that a hopeful neighborhood is where possibilities are the focus. You may now be wondering how to get a handle on what exactly is strong in your own neighborhood. In short, you begin by discovering gifts that you and your neighbors already possess, and that is what we turn to next.

# Share Individual Gifts

## A HOPEFUL NEIGHBORHOOD IS WHERE EVERYONE'S GIFTS ARE SHARED.

*If you look at every flower individually, they look quite miserable. Put them together in a vase and they become a bouquet and that's quite attractive. I think about our community often in that way.*

**HENRI NOUWEN**

S ome people have a simplistic view of neighborhoods. For example, the way real estate agents talk when they're trying to sell a property can give you the impression that a neighborhood is either strong ("highly sought after" is the code language) or it is not ("up and coming" is the nice way they put it).

On the surface this may seem like a common-sense way of categorizing neighborhoods—perhaps you can even place your own neighborhood in one of these two categories. But when you spend time focusing on what is strong, you find that this approach is inherently flawed. It turns out that *every single neighborhood* has its own unique strengths. In order to help you discover what's strong in your own neighborhood (regardless of what a real estate agent might say), you can spend time discovering the individual gifts you and your neighbors already possess.

It's one thing to acknowledge conceptually that everyone is gifted, including you and your neighbors. It's another thing entirely to name the various gifts individuals in the neighborhood have to share. When you start to pay attention to what is strong in your neighborhood, you begin to notice things you've never noticed before. In fact, as you walk down this newly discovered path of possibilities, your view of your neighbors will likely be transformed. You may notice people you've never seen before. You may discover familiar neighbors possess gifts that were previously hidden.

Most of all, you will begin to see your neighbors and yourself as valuable, interdependent partners with individual gifts to share in pursuing the common good in your neighborhood.

> **INDIVIDUAL GIFT:** "any aptitude, innate ability, or acquired skill that can be used to develop the well-being of your neighborhood."

A hopeful neighborhood is one where everyone's individual gifts are shared. But these various gifts can't be shared in an explicit and intentional way until they are noticed, acknowledged, and named.

Part of the nature of gifts, whether we are born with them or acquire them over time through formal training or everyday experience, is that we tend to take them for granted. Sometimes when we share a gift, it feels natural and normal, maybe even effortless. Other times we may be so inattentive to our gift that it doesn't even occur to us to share it for the benefit of the people and place around us.

This is why it is important to get specific and explicit about the individual gifts we and our neighbors have.

A hopeful neighborhood is one where everyone is a gift with gifts to share—where everyone's worth is acknowledged and individual gifts are seen as valuable to the entire neighborhood.

**THE POWER OF SHARING INDIVIDUAL GIFTS**

Go to www.hopefulneighborhood.org/fieldguide to see for yourself how powerful it can be to discover gifts and share them with others. Use the space below to respond to the reflection and discussion prompts in the video:

## EVERYONE IS A GIFT

In an increasingly polarized culture, it is refreshing to focus on people's gifts. The divisive rhetoric around us subtly encourages us to look at people as left or right, conservative or progressive, a smart person (who thinks like I do) or a clueless person (who thinks differently than I do).

This way of looking at and categorizing people can become second nature for us. Without even knowing it's happening, we begin to view people through these limited and cynical lenses. This binary, us-or-them way of viewing people not only limits how we see others but can be dangerous over time, creating a toxic environment conducive to the blossoming of distrust and hate. Eventually we are tempted to dismiss others as "garbage" who have no inherent worth.

Our desire to see communities flourish and their well-being increase is based on our belief in the inherent worth of every person regardless of race, political affiliation, nationality, or creed. In the preface to the Barna report *Better Together: How Christians Can Be a Welcome Influence in Their Neighborhoods*, Tony writes, "In an increasingly polarized age where an 'us vs. them' mentality can convince us that those unlike ourselves are of less worth, this project is anchored in the belief that every human being is knit together by the same God and, as such, has value—a gift from God with gifts to share."[1]

This concept is key to unleashing the power contained within our neighborhoods. Without it we are tempted to vilify, patronize, and diminish the very people who have the gifts needed to pursue the common good in our neighborhoods. Divisive media, partisan politics, and the basic fear of people different from ourselves provide formidable barriers to neighborhood well-being, but when we see past those things that make us different, we can discover a new motivation (one that's becoming increasingly rare): the desire to build up and partner with our fellow human beings.

This is what makes focusing on gifts so powerful. When you begin to view your neighbors through the lens of discovering individual gifts, you can see their inherent worth in a way you haven't before. This not only helps you get a broader view of your neighborhood's many gifts, it also changes how you see people in general.

Spend time focusing on individual gifts and you begin to see every person in your neighborhood as someone with dignity, worth, and something to offer. Each one of your neighbors is a gift to your neighborhood.

## GIFTS TO SHARE

The gifts we are referring to here are the aptitudes, innate abilities, and acquired skills that can be used to develop the well-being of a neighborhood. We are all created to use our gifts to bless others while at the same time receiving blessing from the gifts of those around us. Gifts are meant to be shared—they aren't really gifts if they aren't given. In this way individual gifts are both reciprocal and purposeful.

Our particular approach to these shared gifts focuses on how individual gifts can be used in service of the common good of a neighborhood. The well-being of the neighborhood is the organizing principle in evaluating individual gifts rather than people's passions, interests, or sense of personal fulfillment. Recognizing and naming people's individual gifts is a way of focusing on what is strong in your neighborhood.

In order to make the most complete inventory of gifts possible, it is helpful to work through a list of different types of gifts people can have. As you seek to discover and recognize what gifts you or your neighbors have, consider twelve different types of gifts.

 **TWELVE TYPES OF INDIVIDUAL GIFTS**
Go to www.hopefulneighborhood.org/fieldguide to spend some time exploring the wide variety of individual gifts that are likely already spread throughout your neighborhood. Use the notes sections below to record insights, reflections, or questions about each type of individual gifts.

*Technical gifts* help you perform specific tasks that require a special and refined set of skills. Gifts include craftsmanship, profession-specific knowledge, and acquired skills.

NOTES:

*Interpersonal gifts* help you interact with, care for, and build relationships with others. Gifts include active listening, self-awareness, and empathy.

NOTES:

*Entrepreneurial gifts* help you identify new opportunities, set goals, and design strategies to achieve them. Gifts include analytical thinking, market research, marketing skills, problem-solving, and sales.

NOTES:

*Management gifts* help you manage both tasks and people. Gifts include decision-making, project planning, task delegation, and communication.

NOTES:

*Financial gifts* help you plan, organize, direct, and control financial activities. Gifts include accounting, planning, and attention to detail.

NOTES:

*Critical thinking gifts* help you process data to problem solve or make informed decisions. Gifts include analytical thinking, creativity, data analytics, and decision-making.

NOTES:

*Artistic gifts* help you express yourself in creative and artistic ways. Gifts include all forms of artistic expression, media use, design, composition, and performance.

NOTES:

*Civic gifts* help you make an impact by participating as a citizen within an organized community. Gifts include advocacy, knowledge of political systems, and the ability to critically think about civic and political life.

NOTES:

*Intercultural gifts* help you relate to people from other cultures and social groups. Gifts include language skills, respect for others, and the ability to understand cultural differences.

NOTES:

*Communication gifts* help you communicate with individuals or groups in a clear and engaging way. Gifts include organization of thought, presentation, and storytelling.

NOTES:

*Leadership gifts* help you organize people to reach a shared goal and effectively lead them toward that goal. Gifts include the ability to teach and mentor, flexibility, risk-taking, team-building, and time management.

NOTES:

*Teamwork gifts* help you effectively collaborate with and work alongside others. Gifts include collaboration, communication, empathy, humility, positivity, and problem-solving.

NOTES:

> Use the space below to respond to the reflection and discussion prompts in the video:

## MY OWN INDIVIDUAL GIFTS

Having learned about twelve different types of gifts, you can practice discovering your own individual gifts. Take a first pass by listing any aptitudes, innate abilities, or acquired skills you possess in these areas in figure 2.1.

While many of us may have taken personal inventories in the past to categorize our passions or temperament characteristics, it's a completely different experience to consider what aptitude, innate ability, or acquired skill you have that can be shared with the place and people right around you. It may be fun to gain insight into your temperament, but it is empowering and hopeful to realize the many helpful gifts you have.

## SESSION REVIEW

Continue your pursuit of the common good by taking some specific steps to conceptualize, personalize, and visualize what it would look like to notice, acknowledge, and name the various gifts you and your neighbors have to share with each other.

*Conceptualize.* In your own words, describe some of the various benefits that occur when people share their gifts.

# FIRST LOOK AT INDIVIDUAL GIFTS

| TECHNICAL | INTERPERSONAL |
|---|---|
| ENTREPRENEURIAL | MANAGEMENT |
| FINANCIAL | CRITICAL THINKING |
| ARTISTIC | CIVIC |
| INTERCULTURAL | COMMUNICATION |
| LEADERSHIP | TEAMWORK |

FIGURE 2.1. MY INDIVIDUAL GIFTS

*Personalize.* Having done a first pass at considering what individual gifts you have, do a more thorough pass by taking the EveryGift Inventory. Go to www.hopefulneighborhood.org/everygift to get started. List what you learn about your own gifts and how they could potentially be shared within your neighborhood.

*Visualize.* What individual gifts have you noticed in members of your own household or others in your neighborhood? In what ways might those specific gifts be shared in a way that benefits the neighborhood?

## SUMMARY

We spent this session discovering that a hopeful neighborhood is one where everyone's gifts are shared. You may already have a sense, though, that your individual gifts and those of your neighbors aren't the only gifts to be found in your neighborhood. In fact, your neighborhood has many other types of gifts just waiting to be discovered. That is what we turn to next.

# Value Neighborhood Uniqueness

## A HOPEFUL NEIGHBORHOOD IS WHERE NEIGHBORS VALUE THEIR NEIGHBORHOOD'S UNIQUENESS.

*The citizen takes his city for granted far too often. He forgets to marvel.*

**CARLOS FUENTES**

No matter how much you currently appreciate your neighborhood, the process of noticing and naming all the gifts to be found there will likely increase your affection for where you live.

In the Spring of 2000, Red Wassenich, a librarian living in Austin, Texas, called in to a local radio show and happened to make an offhand comment about the radio station doing its part to "keep Austin weird."

Because of Red's love for his hometown, the phrase stuck with him and he began putting the words "Keep Austin Weird" on bumper stickers. The phrase caught on, showing up on various signs through Austin and, eventually, it was adopted as the official slogan of Austin.

To Red's chagrin, the slogan would eventually be used as a marketing tool, but at its core it was born out of Red's appreciation for the many gifts Austin possesses and his love for his unique city. Not only did Red recognize that his city was unique, he *valued* that uniqueness—he wanted to "keep it" unique.

Red is not the only person, of course, to recognize and appreciate the uniqueness of where he lives. In fact, the phrase he coined about his beloved Austin would eventually be adopted in Portland, Oregon (in 2003), in Louisville (2005), in Indianapolis (2013), and elsewhere. When you pay attention to where you live—to your community's own set of gifts and its particular history—you can't help but be struck by how unique it is. It turns out every place is unique and there is something powerful about recognizing and valuing that uniqueness.

Whether you're talking about a city, a town, or a neighborhood, it is not uncommon for the residents of a place to recognize and ultimately value what is unique about where they live. There's a neighborhood near us in St. Louis, Maplewood, that has adapted Red's phrase with a little twist: "Keep MapleWeird." At the end of the day the folks who live in Maplewood are experts on Maplewood: they know its streets, stores, homes, culture, groups, characters, celebrations, traditions . . . all of it. And they like it!

Something special happens when neighbors not only recognize the various unique gifts of their neighborhood but value them as well. You may find this happening to you as you continue to focus on possibilities in your own neighborhood—not only will your vision of your neighbors be transformed, but you will begin to see your neighborhood in a new light as well.

Local restaurants aren't just convenient; they are social hubs and economic drivers. The corner park isn't just where you walk your dog; it's a place where neighborhood kids play and the community is rejuvenated. In these and other ways you will begin to notice how uniquely gifted your neighborhood is—in its history, its people, and even its location.

**THE POWER OF FALLING IN LOVE WITH YOUR NEIGHBORHOOD**

Go to www.hopefulneighborhood.org/fieldguide to see for yourself how powerful it can be to recognize what's unique about your neighborhood. Use the space below to respond to the reflection and discussion prompts in the video:

## YOUR NEIGHBORHOOD'S UNIQUE SET OF GIFTS

One of the first obstacles you may face in recognizing the many gifts all around you is the fact that you are accustomed to your neighborhood. In fact, the longer you have lived in there, the more tempting it may be to take what is unique and valuable about your neighborhood for granted.

None of us is immune to this. Don remembers moving from Texas to Oregon just before his freshman year of high school. Coming from a desert, he couldn't help but be amazed by the vivid shades of green everywhere, the refreshing creeks and streams that cut through town, and the breathtaking views of snowcapped Mt. Hood in the distance. But what was perhaps most shocking was how "home-blind" many of his neighbors had become to these natural gifts—they had been around this lush beauty for so long that they stopped noticing it.

All of us can be like Don's neighbors in Oregon: we become so familiar with the various features of our own neighborhood that we take valuable gifts for granted or, worse, stop noticing them at all. This is why it's important to spend time looking at neighborhood gifts and creating a basic asset map. This can help you catalogue the wide variety of gifts spread all throughout your neighborhood.

We've already considered how you and your neighbors each have individual gifts just waiting to be discovered and used to pursue the common good. But there are other types of neighborhood gifts God has blessed you and your neighbors with as well.

> **NEIGHBORHOOD GIFTS:** "any asset in your zip code or adjacent zip code that can be used to develop the well-being of your neighborhood."

These neighborhood gifts include group, physical, and associational assets as well as gifts found in the private, public, and nonprofit sectors. Part of what makes your neighborhood unique is its own distinctive mix of these gifts.

>  **SIX TYPES OF NEIGHBORHOOD GIFTS**
>
> Go to www.hopefulneighborhood.org /fieldguide to get a basic introduction to these six important types of neighborhood gifts. Use the notes sections below to record insights, reflections, or questions about each type of neighborhood gifts.

*Group gifts* include the people groups that add to the cultural richness of your neighborhood; for example, local artists and musicians, immigrant populations, children and youth, college students, and senior citizens.

**NOTES:**

*Physical gifts* include natural or manmade physical features that you and your neighbors use in your neighborhood; for example, parks and trails, streets and lights, community centers or gardens, and meeting or artistic venues.

NOTES:

*Associational gifts* include the volunteer groups, clubs, or associations that various neighbors belong to; for example, local neighborhood organizations, community groups and clubs, and demographically specific groups.

NOTES:

*Private sector gifts* include the businesses or business groups located in your neighborhood; for example, local retailers, restaurants, banks, media outlets, chambers of commerce, business associations, and private schools.

NOTES:

*Public sector gifts* include public agencies and facilities that operate within your neighborhood; for example, government agencies, first responders, public schools or colleges, public hospitals or clinics, municipal libraries, pools, and golf courses.

NOTES:

*Nonprofit sector gifts* include programs, facilities, and services provided in your neighborhood by nonprofit organizations; for example, religious organizations, housing shelters, food kitchens, health clinics, and counseling centers.

NOTES:

Use the space below to respond to the reflection and discussion prompts in the video:

## DISCOVERING YOUR NEIGHBORHOOD'S GIFTS

There are three basic ways of discovering the various gifts your neighborhood has been blessed with: recall, reconnaissance, and research. Each of these discovery techniques can help you build out a more thorough inventory of the many neighborhood gifts surrounding you.

**Recall.** This is the process of discovering gifts you already know about from your own experience. It's as simple as listing out gifts in each of the six categories from memory—something you can do by yourself right where you are.

**Reconnaissance.** Reconnaissance is the process of discovering gifts through observation. You can hunt around for gifts by walking or driving through your neighborhood, by informally chatting with neighbors about their experience, or even by searching the internet for basic information on your neighborhood.

# FIRST LOOK AT NEIGHBORHOOD GIFTS

| GROUP GIFTS | PHYSICAL GIFTS |
|---|---|
| | |
| ASSOCIATIONAL GIFTS | PRIVATE SECTOR GIFTS |
| | |
| PUBLIC SECTOR GIFTS | NONPROFIT SECTOR GIFTS |
| | |

FIGURE 3.1. MY NEIGHBORHOOD'S GIFTS

*Research.* Research is the process of discovering gifts by looking
at data about your neighborhood. This data could come from for-
mally surveying your neighbors, examining community databases
(often organized online by zip code), or reading books or articles
about your neighborhood.

Let's start with recall. Based on what you already know, list the
various gifts your neighborhood has in each of these six areas in
figure 3.1.

## YOUR NEIGHBORHOOD'S UNIQUE HISTORY

Your neighborhood's particular set of gifts is only one part of what
makes your neighborhood unique. Every neighborhood also has a
history. And whether that history is long or short, calm or eventful, it's
an important part of what makes your neighborhood what it is today.

Getting to know the history of your neighborhood (and the community your neighborhood sits within) is an important part of recognizing and valuing your neighborhood's uniqueness. In your work
to uncover more about the unique history of your own neighborhood, it's important to recognize that history is always complex.
It's also important to seek out a variety of perspectives on that
complex history.

Don once lived in the East Palo Alto neighborhood in the Bay Area
of California. When he first moved there, he began to slowly learn
about the history of the neighborhood from his neighbors. Many of
his neighbors, independently, wanted to share the story of how the
local high school had been shut down (for lack of funding) and began
to be used as a food bank.

It became clear to Don that while the food bank was an important
nonprofit sector gift in the community, the fact that it was housed
in the empty high school building kept the wound of the school
closure fresh for his neighbors. It would have been impossible to
fully understand East Palo Alto at that time or the work of the food
bank or the community's almost defensive passion for education

without learning about the complex history of the neighborhood and surrounding community.

For you to understand your own neighborhood's uniqueness, you will need to become something of an amateur historian. Talking with neighbors, reading histories, and asking lots of questions will help you learn about your own neighborhood's complex history.

An important part of this work is listening to and learning from a diversity of people. Someone's age, race, or class definitely affects how they experience events that have taken place. For example, Don found that those with children experienced the closing of the high school in East Palo Alto differently than those who didn't have children. African Americans and Latinos experienced the closure (and subsequent busing of students to a mostly White school in Palo Alto) differently than White residents.

While your search through history will undoubtedly uncover delightful, joyful events from the past, know that you may also uncover real pain and trauma as well. Understanding trauma is not about discovering what's wrong with a person or community; it's about understanding how events are experienced and the lasting effect those events have on the health and well-being of those who went through them. In 2014, the Trauma and Justice Strategic Initiative of the US Department of Health and Human Services developed a simple "Three E's" model that can help us better understand trauma.

**TRAUMA:** "a lasting adverse impact on the health and well-being of individuals, relationships, communities, and societies (from the Greek word for 'wound')."

Understanding trauma in your neighborhood is important. When you are pursuing the common good, trauma can be an unseen barrier. Without understanding the history of individuals and their communities, even the best intentions can unintentionally deepen existing trauma or create additional trauma.

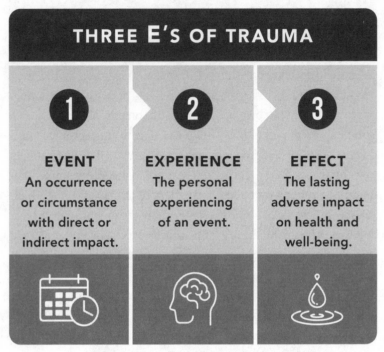

**FIGURE 3.2. UNDERSTANDING TRAUMA**

Beginning to recognize your neighborhood's unique history and its particular set of gifts will help you, over time, begin to marvel at your neighborhood and value its uniqueness.

## SESSION REVIEW

Continue your pursuit of the common good by taking some specific steps to conceptualize, personalize, and visualize what it would look like to recognize and value the uniqueness of your own neighborhood.

*Conceptualize.* Restate in your own words the various changes that occur when residents begin to value their neighborhood's uniqueness.

*Personalize.* As we've seen, people in Austin, Portland, Louisville, Indianapolis, and elsewhere like how "weird" their unique community is and want to keep it that way. Reflecting on your own neighborhood and its history, list some of the most obvious features that make it "weird" and unique:

*Visualize.* Having taken the first step of discovering your neighborhood's gifts (through recall), go back to your First Look at Neighborhood Gifts (figure 3.1) and fill it out more fully by taking the second step: reconnaissance. Spend some time making observations about your neighborhood while walking, driving, informally chatting with neighbors, or exploring basic information online.

List new gifts you discover below (or add them straight to figure 3.1):

## SUMMARY

We spent this session discovering that a hopeful neighborhood is where neighbors value their neighborhood's uniqueness. Three sessions in, you may be asking this question: If I am focusing on possibilities, discovering individual gifts, and valuing my neighborhood's uniqueness, what does that actually get me or my neighborhood? That is what we will discuss next.

# Long for Neighborhood Well-Being

## A HOPEFUL NEIGHBORHOOD IS WHERE NEIGHBORS LONG FOR THEIR NEIGHBORHOOD'S WELL-BEING.

*I believe that the community—in the fullest sense: a place and all its creatures—is the smallest unit of health and that to speak of the health of an isolated individual is a contradiction in terms.*

**WENDELL BERRY**

B y this point you may be wondering where we are heading. Where, exactly, does this path of possibilities lead? In short, the path of possibilities leads to a hopeful neighborhood—a place where neighbors work together to pursue neighborhood well-being. For neighborhoods, well-being is ultimately the highest form of common good.

**WELL-BEING:** "a positive state of being in which individuals and groups thrive and flourish."

As Wendell Berry suggests, well-being is ultimately a communal thing. While we are accustomed to thinking about the health of an individual, it may be new to some of us to think about the health of a neighborhood.

The idea of "neighborhood well-being" gets at the very real inter-connectedness that exists between us and the people and place where we live. As the poet John Donne famously expressed:

No man is an island, / Entire of itself; / Every man is a piece of the continent, / A part of the main.

Whether we recognize it or not, none of us is an island. We and our neighbors and everything in our neighborhood are inextricably con-nected. In fact, the American Hospital Association came to a similar conclusion in 2018:

A growing volume of evidence shows that one's personal health is influenced not only by genetics and other biological charac-teristics but also by a variety of social factors. . . . These social determinants of health typically strongly correlate with the health status of a given community, so much so that we now believe that your zip code can be a very accurate predictor of your health.[1]

Tony is the proud father of his first and only son, Ben. Ben was born in an Illinois town across the river from St. Louis. The town was home to hundreds of hardworking people, many of whom found em-ployment in the local steel plant.

That steel plant was the heart of the community. Without it, the citizens and the city would suffer financial pain. The people and the plant were connected in a very tangible way, not only financially, but also physically for some.

This was the case with Ben. Not long after his birth, Ben started to develop what appeared to be asthma. And while there are several reasons for asthma to occur, one of the causes frequently referenced is the quality of air in one's town and surrounding areas.

Not long after, Tony and his family moved to another town and Ben's breathing issues cleared. It was an important lesson in how in-tertwined the well-being of a place and its people can be.

Neighborhood well-being is a measure of the corporate or communal health of a neighborhood. In a hopeful neighborhood neighbors are not only mindful of this communal well-being; they are passionate about it. They want their neighborhood to reach a state of well-being. In fact, their neighborhood's well-being is something they actively long for and therefore strive toward.

 **THE POWER OF THINKING ABOUT NEIGHBORHOOD WELL-BEING**

Go to www.hopefulneighborhood.org/fieldguide to see for yourself how powerful it can be to think about the interconnected nature of your own neighborhood. Use the space below to respond to the reflection and discussion prompts in the video:

## WHAT, EXACTLY, ARE WE LONGING FOR?

But what determines the well-being of your neighborhood? You can think of your neighborhood as you would think of a person. A person's well-being is holistic—it includes their physical health, emotional health, mental health, and more.

In the same way, your neighborhood's well-being comprises a complex tapestry of interrelated factors that work together to create not only an environment but a state of being for those who reside within it.

How can you assess all of these interrelated factors? By looking carefully at your neighborhood.

Tony grew up in Downs, a small rural farming community in Illinois. And while this was long before the age of social media, local news websites, and daily email updates, the goings-on in the community could still be easily known.

The only technology needed back then was a comfy chair and the front living room window. Whoever sat in the chair and looked through the window became the news anchor for the home. You knew when the farmers were coming home from the field, who got a new car and how fast they were driving it, which neighbor's health was waning, and who had visitors in from out of town.

While Tony would tease his mother from time to time about "spying" on the neighbors, there was a certain comfort knowing that other neighbors were doing the same thing from their comfy chairs and living room windows. You can learn a lot about a neighborhood when you learn to look carefully with loving and watchful eyes. The truth is, no matter where you live you can learn to "look carefully" at your own neighborhood.

To help you do this we have developed the Well-Being Window, a simple model that can help you become curious and attentive to all the various aspects of well-being in your own neighborhood.

## THE WELL-BEING WINDOW

The Well-Being Window has four different panes, or quadrants, if you will. Each one of these quadrants gives you a distinct and important view of your neighborhood. Taken together, these four quadrants can give you a more comprehensive picture of your neighborhood than you would otherwise have.

You look through quadrant one to become more curious and attentive about the well-being of the actual *people* in your neighborhood: What is their physical, emotional, and intellectual health?

By looking through quadrant two you get a sense of the various *relationships* that exist among people, as well as the social, cultural, and vocational health of those relationships.

Quadrant three is about the overall *environment*: the natural, infrastructural, and residential health of your neighborhood.

## THE WELL-BEING WINDOW
### WITH NEIGHBORHOOD HEALTH INDICATORS

| PEOPLE | RELATIONSHIPS |
|---|---|
| **Q1** | **Q2** |
| Physical, Emotional, and Intellectual Health | Social, Cultural, and Vocational Health |
| **ENVIRONMENT** | **SYSTEMS** |
| **Q3** | **Q4** |
| Natural, Infrastructural, and Residential Health | Political, Economic, and Associational Health |

**FIGURE 4.1. THE WELL-BEING WINDOW**

Finally, by looking through quadrant four you consider the well-being of the various *systems* that are present within and around your neighborhood, including the political, economic, and associational health of your neighborhood.

As you look through each quadrant of the Well-Being Window you can gain a broader palette for thinking about your neighborhood in these twelve important areas of health. Each of these twelve neighborhood health indicators is important, and viewed together they can give you a fuller, more nuanced sense of your neighborhood's overall health.

Gaining this more nuanced sense of the relative health of your neighborhood's people, relationships, environment, and systems can help you dream in bigger and better and more practical ways for your neighborhood.

**TWELVE NEIGHBORHOOD HEALTH INDICATORS**

Go to www.hopefulneighborhood.org/fieldguide to learn more about these twelve important areas of neighborhood health. Use the notes sections below to record insights, reflections, or questions about each neighborhood health indicator.

## QUADRANT ONE: PEOPLE

*Physical health* refers to the state of biological functioning that allows individuals to live and thrive. Investments in physical health include education, self-care, and personal improvement.

NOTES:

*Emotional health* refers to the state of mental functioning that allows individuals to understand, communicate, and manage emotions. Investments in emotional health include education, self-care, and personal improvement.

NOTES:

*Intellectual health* refers to the state of mental functioning that allows individuals to develop knowledge, creativity, and innovation needed to solve problems. Investments in intellectual health include education, self-care, and personal improvement.

NOTES:

## QUADRANT TWO: RELATIONSHIPS

*Social health* refers to the presence of meaningful interactions that provide support, encouragement, and belonging in your neighborhood, as well as the level of participation in those interactions. Indicators of social health include acceptance, cohesion, inclusion, and equality.

NOTES:

*Cultural health* refers to an environment supportive of the diversity of people and their customs, traditions, heritage, and beliefs. Indicators of cultural health include tolerance, awareness, and appreciation.

NOTES:

*Vocational health* refers to how well people are functioning in their various work and career roles. Indicators of vocational health include acceptance, agency, stability, flexibility, and resilience.

NOTES:

## QUADRANT THREE: ENVIRONMENTAL

*Natural health* refers to the condition of the local physical ecosystem. Indicators of natural health include quality, stability, and biodiversity.

NOTES:

*Infrastructural health* refers to the state of public systems and utilities necessary for the support of a community and its people. Indicators of infrastructural health include well-functioning sewers, roads, transportation services, amenities, internet, and built assets.

NOTES:

*Residential health* refers to the quality of the spaces designed for housing. Indicators of residential health include stability, quality, equity, accessibility, and affordability.

NOTES:

## QUADRANT FOUR: SYSTEMS

*Political health* refers to the condition of the political structures that govern and direct public affairs. Indicators of political health include civic participation, accountability, legitimacy, fairness, and equity.

NOTES:

*Economic health* refers to the production, consumption, and management of wealth and resources. Indicators of economic health include growth, commerce, production, and employment.

NOTES:

*Associational health* refers to the presence of groups that rely on volunteers to work toward achieving a common goal, as well as participation in these groups. Indicators of associational health include membership, activity, and variety.

NOTES:

Use the space below to respond to the reflection and discussion prompts in the video:

## ASSESSING NEIGHBORHOOD HEALTH

In order to understand the current well-being of your own neighborhood, it's important to assess each of these twelve neighborhood health indicators. This may seem overwhelming at first, but you can do it using the same simple, three-step process we used to look for gifts in your neighborhood:

- Recall (what you already know from your own experience)
- Reconnaissance (what you can learn through observation)
- Research (what you can learn by looking at the data)

Recall is something you can do on your own, based on your current experience. In some areas your experience will give you lots to go on. For example, if you have children in the public schools, you will have some great insights on intellectual health.

Reconnaissance helps you widen your base of knowledge through observation. If you don't have children in the schools, you could take a walk around the local schools to see what you can see or talk with a neighbor who has children.

Research allows you to access objective data, which will help you assess neighborhood health even more. You could find out, for example, what graduation rates are for your neighborhood schools or what the average test scores are.

Through recall, reconnaissance, and research you can assess all twelve health indicators for your own neighborhood. And don't be surprised if this process naturally creates a longing within you for even greater neighborhood well-being. You may find yourself contemplating various possibilities; for example, how an area of strong health can be built upon or leveraged to increase other areas of health. Assessing health tends to plant hopeful seeds in this way.

## SESSION REVIEW

Continue your pursuit of the common good by taking some specific steps to conceptualize, personalize, and visualize what it would look like to long for the well-being of your neighborhood.

*Conceptualize.* In your own words, describe how the well-being of a neighborhood can affect (and be affected by) those who live in the neighborhood.

*Personalize.* Based on what you already know about your neighborhood, how would you rate (on a scale of one to ten) your neighborhood's well-being for each quadrant? Use figure 4.2 to record your answers.

*Visualize.* To further nurture an inner longing for well-being in your own neighborhood, choose three neighborhood health indicators and dream about what greater well-being in those areas could look like in your neighborhood. Write out an aspirational description for each below.

1.


2.


3.

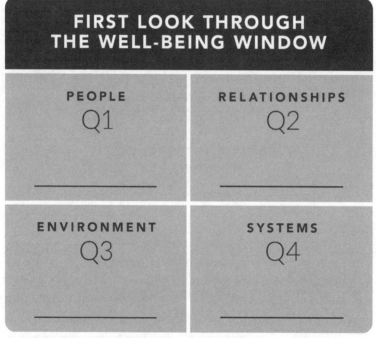

FIGURE 4.2. MY NEIGHBORHOOD'S WELL-BEING

## SUMMARY

We spent this session discovering that a hopeful neighborhood is where neighbors long for their neighborhood's well-being. As you tap into that longing, you will likely get excited about possible futures for your neighborhood, and that is exactly what we take up next.

Session
Five

# Imagine Possibilities Collaboratively

## A HOPEFUL NEIGHBORHOOD IS WHERE NEIGHBORS COLLABORATIVELY IMAGINE POSSIBILITIES.

*If you have an apple and I have an apple and we exchange these apples then you and I will still each have one apple. But if you have an idea and I have an idea and we exchange these ideas, then each of us will have two ideas.*

**CHARLES F. BRANNAN**

Since the beginning of this field guide we have been inexorably heading toward possibilities. Rather than focusing on problems in our neighborhoods (and trying to fix them), we have been focusing on possibilities: specific paths toward greater neighborhood well-being that rely on current gifts in the neighborhood.

Now that we have discovered more about the gifts embedded in our own neighborhoods and have a more robust picture of neighborhood well-being, how do we imagine the right path forward?

In short, we can choose a path toward greater neighborhood well-being by imagining possibilities collaboratively. A hopeful neighborhood is where neighbors work together to imagine possibilities.

**COLLABORATE:** "to work jointly with others; literally, to co-labor."

Even if you as an individual did all of the activities called for in the first four sessions of this field guide, you would still not be in a place to discern the path forward for your neighborhood. No single individual can imagine all possibilities, especially not the best or most helpful ones—we do our best thinking with others. Only together can we imagine the right path forward for our neighborhood.

Don once lived in a very beautiful, very remote neighborhood on Mt. Rainier in Paradise, Washington. One day he and a friend, Chris, went on an extended backpacking trip. They hiked across glaciers, camped in valleys filled with flowers, and ate off the land.

Each step of the way, Don was struck by how much he and Chris were relying on each other. On their first night of camping, Don pulled out some apples he had brought along, expecting a simple, cold dinner. But Chris pulled out his pocketknife and started cutting and folding a soda can he had just emptied, turning it into a small pan in which they proceeded to boil cut-up apple pieces. Don loved the warm meal and went to sleep thankful he had someone to partner with on the trail.

Don was even more thankful the next day when he and Chris got terribly lost. Neither Don nor Chris knew the way back home. At times they each thought they knew the right path, but it was only by eventually putting their minds together that they were able to figure out the correct route back.

At one point, Don (who was just learning how to read topographical maps) pointed out that the map showed there should be a river on the ridge they were standing on. Chris, who actually knew how to read the map, was able to correct Don. At another point, Chris (who was legally blind) argued strongly that they should follow some tracks in the snow. Don, who could clearly see that the tracks were made by a bear, recommended otherwise.

It was only by working collaboratively that Don and Chris were able to have a warm meal and find the path home. Collaboration protects us from the dangers of trying to go it alone.

The same is true in pursuing the common good of our neighborhoods: it is by working together with our neighbors, rather than going it alone, that we will be able to imagine hopeful, helpful possibilities.

 **THE POWER OF COLLABORATION**
Go to www.hopefulneighborhood.org/fieldguide to see for yourself how powerful it can be to collaborate with others. Use the space below to respond to the reflection and discussion prompts in the video:

## A FUSION OF HORIZONS

The reality is, whether you are trying to find a mountain path home or discover a possible way forward for your neighborhood, you are limited by what you personally can see. Your experience, your education, and your context will naturally define a horizon of possibilities that you can see from where you stand.

German philosopher Hans-Georg Gadamer argued that all human beings are naturally limited and biased in what they can see on their own—they are naturally "prejudiced" by their own experiences. This means we each have a certain horizon within which we can imagine possibilities for our neighborhood.

But something special happens when we stand side by side with others and share our personal perspectives and experiences: we experience what Gadamer called a "fusion of horizons." Together

## WHAT I SEE

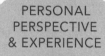

PERSONAL
PERSPECTIVE
& EXPERIENCE

PERSONAL
PERSPECTIVE
& EXPERIENCE

**FIGURE 5.1. HORIZON**

## WHAT WE SEE

PERSONAL
PERSPECTIVE
& EXPERIENCE

PERSONAL
PERSPECTIVE
& EXPERIENCE

FUSION
OF
HORIZONS

**FIGURE 5.2. SHARED HORIZON**

our perspectives are widened, and we can imagine more possibilities than any one of us could alone.

Up on Mt. Rainier Don couldn't understand the map, but he could see far distances. Chris could interpret the map correctly, but he couldn't see well. They each had a naturally limited horizon. But together they had a much more expanded horizon. And by collaborating, they were able to find their way back home.

Likewise, by this point in the field guide you can likely see a certain horizon of possibilities for your neighborhood. Maybe your work on the gifts and uniqueness of your neighborhood has given you some great ideas. Perhaps reflecting on your neighborhood's well-being has offered you a more nuanced understanding of where things stand now.

You have a certain horizon that allows you to see (and even get excited about) a certain set of possibilities. What your horizon reveals is important and valuable. Nevertheless, you have limitations and biases. There will be parts of your neighborhood that you are blind to. There will be dynamics among neighbors that you can't quite understand.

But something special will happen if you stand side by side with a few neighbors and imagine possibilities for your neighborhood together. Your shared perspective will naturally be wider and include possibilities none of you ever would have thought of alone.

## COLLABORATING ACROSS CULTURES

Part of what defines your horizon is your unique set of cultural influences. This is the case for everyone. Whether you recognize it or not, you are profoundly shaped by your culture—and your neighbors are profoundly shaped by their cultures as well. This is part of what makes partnering crossculturally so powerful: you get a much wider shared horizon when you collaborate with people who have a different culture than you have.

Don noticed this back in East Palo Alto—he didn't have a full and accurate understanding of the food bank in town until he had talked with people from a variety of cultures. The more people he talked with, the wider their shared horizon became.

Collaborating across cultures is powerful, but it requires learning how to appreciate cultural differences. Anthropologist and crosscultural researcher Edward T. Hall's important work in this area underscored how complex cultures are and how important it is to consider both surface and deep aspects of culture. If you want to get the most out of crosscultural collaboration, you will need to explore *surface* culture (which you can observe) and *deep* culture (which takes time to discover).

 **UNDERSTANDING CULTURE**

Go to www.hopefulneighborhood.org/fieldguide to learn more about observable *surface* culture and discoverable *deep* culture. Use the space below to respond to the reflection and discussion prompts in the video:

## IMAGINING POSSIBILITIES TOGETHER

The path of focusing on possibilities (including discovering individual gifts, valuing your neighborhood's uniqueness, and longing for neighborhood well-being) will naturally lead you to imagine hopeful possibilities for your neighborhood. Ideas will naturally flow.

But collaboration is something you must choose. We naturally assume we see everything there is to see—it is an act of will to admit we have a limited horizon. We naturally assume our ideas take everything into account—it is an act of will to gather with others, honestly consider their ideas, and add your ideas to the group. We naturally gravitate toward people who are like us—it is an act of will to intentionally cross cultures and collaborate with people who are different than we are.

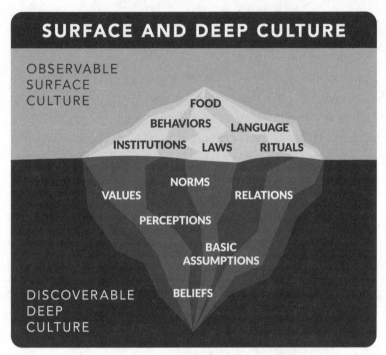

**FIGURE 5.3. THE ICEBERG MODEL OF CULTURE**

The decision to imagine possibilities collaboratively may seem costly and inefficient at times, but the payoff is worth it. Together with your neighbors you will be able to imagine amazing possibilities together.

## SESSION REVIEW

Continue your pursuit of the common good by taking some specific steps to conceptualize, personalize, and visualize what it would look like to collaboratively imagine possibilities with your neighbors.

*Conceptualize.* In your own words, describe some of the important dynamics to keep in mind when collaborating across cultures with neighbors.

*Personalize.* Collaboration takes time, energy, and a personal investment but is incredibly rewarding. How have you experienced both the challenges and benefits of collaboration in your own life?

*Visualize.* As we've seen, there is something powerful about collaborating with people who are different from you. As you think about your neighborhood, who are some people different from you (whether because of age, race, or class) that you could imagine discussing your neighborhood with?

## SUMMARY

We spent this session discovering that a hopeful neighborhood is where neighbors collaboratively imagine possibilities. But if you imagine enough possibilities, you are eventually going to want to pick one and do something about it. Let's look at that step next.

# Create and Work a Plan

## A HOPEFUL NEIGHBORHOOD IS WHERE NEIGHBORS CREATE AND WORK A PLAN TOGETHER.

*Do not live entirely isolated, having retreated into yourselves, as if you were already [fully] justified, but gather instead to seek together the common good.*

**SAINT BARNABAS**

At a restaurant in Sausalito, California, in 1982, Anne Herbert did a very small thing that wound up having a very large impact. She wrote eight words on a placemat: "Practice random kindness and senseless acts of beauty."

Anne was responding to the common phrase "random violence and senseless acts of cruelty"; she flipped it on its head in a clever way that eventually made its way onto bumper stickers and into the vernacular.

There is something beautiful and inspiring about "practicing random kindness"—especially when compared with random violence! And undoubtedly there is much good that can come of small acts of kindness right in our own neighborhoods.

But in this session, we are considering acts of neighborhood kindness that are not random at all. We're considering doing something in your neighborhood that is thoughtful and purposeful and premeditated.

A hopeful neighborhood is where neighbors create and work a plan together. Plans are where the rubber meets the road and where aspiration and inspiration produce a harvest of well-being in the neighborhood.

Everything we've talked about so far (focusing on possibilities, sharing individual gifts, valuing neighborhood uniqueness, longing for neighborhood well-being, and imagining possibilities collaboratively) are a lead-up to this important lesson: the power of gathering with others to create and work a plan. Being random can bless your neighbors, but being planful can transform your neighborhood.

The early Christian writer Barnabas was onto something when he encouraged the first generations of Christians in Alexandria, Egypt, not to isolate themselves or retreat from their neighbors. But notice that there is a sense of intentionality implied in his encouragement to "gather" with others to "seek together" the common good. Gathering with others and seeking something together will necessarily involve some sort of coordination or planning.

Random acts of kindness may be a great starting place, but gathering together with others to intentionally seek the common good has more legs. Creating and working a plan can lead to long-term, lasting well-being within a neighborhood.

Tony's first real experience with working toward the good of his neighborhood started with attending the Neighborhood Leadership Academy at a local college. Surrounded by dozens of people who had a heart for their communities, he was amazed and inspired to hear what other classmates were working on to increase their community's well-being. While sharing their passions, gifts, and creativity were some of the highlights of the evening course, one lesson rang loud and true: passion without a plan will fail.

Tony's classmates helped him learn the importance of being intentional while pursuing well-being. It would take time, planning, communication, buy-in, and trust. Each of the exciting visions presented by his fellow students would need to be broken down into manageable steps that were properly resourced and tracked before the future they imagined could become a reality. But when they did this, when they intentionally pursued the common good, each step brought them closer to translating the possibilities they imagined into a reality they could see.

 **THE POWER OF A PLAN**

Go to www.hopefulneighborhood.org/ fieldguide to see for yourself how powerful it can be to intentionally plan for the sake of your neighborhood. Use the space below to respond to the reflection and discussion prompts in the video:

## TAKING THE INITIATIVE

In most cases, neighbors don't spontaneously gather together and seek after the common good of their neighborhood. There is usually a spark or nudge or encouragement from one or two neighbors that precipitates hopeful gathering and seeking.

Our nationwide research on neighborhood communities of action confirms the important role of these founders. Founders are like their neighbors in most ways: they live in the neighborhood, they have regular jobs, they don't have formal training in community development or organizing. What makes a founder stand out is simply their willingness to take the initiative.

**FOUNDERS:** "people who gather their neighbors together to seek the common good of their neighborhood."

The founder is willing to wave their hands and ask, "Hey, should we do something to love our neighborhood together?" Helping gather neighbors together necessarily involves some simple organizing. For example, in our research we found that a majority of communities of action meet in person at an appointed or regular time.[1] A founder is willing to help coordinate that time.

This kind of basic initiative and organizing is important. Neighbors rarely get together without such a nudge, and our research shows that more successful neighborhood groups are well-organized.[2] Founders don't have all the answers; they just aren't willing to settle for random acts of kindness—so they stand up, take the initiative, and call their neighbors together. Perhaps you are that person in your neighborhood.

## GATHERING A GROUP OF NEIGHBORS

The invitation to be a founder is not an invitation to be a general or lone wolf or do all the work. It's the invitation to be a neighbor who gathers others. Gathering together with neighbors is important. Remember the invitation from ancient Barnabas: don't be isolated or retreat into yourself. Seeking the common good of your neighborhood is not solo work—it is best entered into as a team sport.

Ideally, if you take the initiative, a small group of your neighbors will come together to create a plan and work that plan. That kind of planful partnership, of course, takes a fair amount of commitment. And not every one of your neighbors will be ready to commit to partner with you in that way.

It's important to remember that that's okay. As you can see in the Participation Funnel in figure 6.1, there are natural steps people take in getting more and more involved in something new. Elias St. Elmo Lewis first described this funnel-like process over a century ago and this natural progression can be seen in a variety of fields. The truth is there is a variety of ways your neighbors can join in the fun of pursuing the common good of the neighborhood.

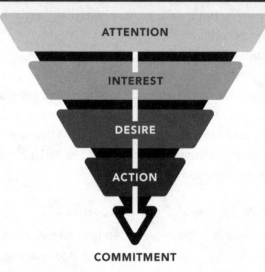

**FIGURE 6.1. THE PARTICIPATION FUNNEL**

Some of your neighbors may take an interest in pursuing the common good of the neighborhood but never actually develop a desire to do anything about it. Other neighbors may desire to make a difference in the neighborhood but need help figuring out how to take action. Some of your neighbors may want to take action with you, using their own gifts in the process, but may not want to be involved in planning.

But some of your neighbors will be ready to make a commitment to enter into the process right alongside you.

## WHAT'S YOUR PROCESS?

So, what exactly is the best process for neighbors to use when creating and working a plan? If you were focusing on problems in your neighborhood, then your process for developing a plan would be simple enough:

1. Identify a problem.

2. Come up with a solution.

3. Implement the solution.

But as we've already seen, a deficit-based approach can be problematic and is likely to produce a plan that may cause more problems than it actually fixes.

Instead, you need a process that incorporates all of the lessons we've learned so far, a process that focuses you and your neighbors on possibilities, not problems. You need a process that will produce a specific and actionable plan based on what is strong in your neighborhood, not on what is wrong. In short, you need a process that looks more like this:

1. Discover the gifts.

2. Imagine the possibilities.

3. Pursue the common good.

This discover-imagine-pursue process is based on all the lessons we've considered so far and sets you and your neighbors up not to do random acts of kindness but to do planful acts that promote the common good of your neighborhood. Each step of this process is important.

Discovering the gifts that are already there in your neighborhood requires *curiosity*. You discover gifts by looking for them: in yourself, in your neighbors, and all throughout your neighborhood. This part of the process will likely grow and cultivate your curiosity about the people and place right around you.

Imagining possibilities requires *creativity*. After spending time discovering the gifts around us, we naturally begin daydreaming about what all those gifts might mean. Imagining the possibilities is a collaborative effort that is part strategy, part brainstorming, and part inspiration. It's about noticing connections and potential synergies.

The final part of the process, pursuing the common good, requires *careful plans*. Seeking to improve the well-being of your neighborhood is no small thing: it lifts you out of the realm of randomness and

## THE HOPEFUL NEIGHBORHOOD PROCESS

**1**    **DISCOVER** the Gifts

**2**    **IMAGINE** the Possibilities

**3**    **PURSUE** the Common Good

**FIGURE 6.2. THE HOPEFUL NEIGHBORHOOD PROJECT'S THREE-STEP PROCESS**

 **THE HOPEFUL NEIGHBORHOOD PROCESS**

Go to www.hopefulneighborhood.org/fieldguide to learn more about this important discover-imagine-pursue process used by members of the supportive Hopeful Neighborhood Network. Use the space that follows to respond to the reflection and discussion prompts in the video:

pushes you to stand side by side with gifted neighbors in a planful sort of way as you strive together for the sake of your neighborhood.

That's it: discover, imagine, pursue. This basic three-step process can help you develop a specific, tangible plan for intentionally pursuing the common good right where you live—just as it has for people just like you all across the country.

## SESSION REVIEW

Continue your pursuit of the common good by taking some specific steps to conceptualize, personalize, and visualize what it would look like to be a founder, to take the initiative to help your neighbors create and work a plan together.

*Conceptualize.* Compare and contrast random acts of kindness with an intentional pursuit of the common good.

*Personalize.* Founders are willing to be the first people to "wave their hands" and invite their neighbors to gather and consider seeking after the common good of the neighborhood. As you consider being a founder, what excites you most about doing that in your own neighborhood?

What barriers to being a founder do you feel?

*Visualize.* Based on our research on neighborhood groups we have developed a helpful, flexible, tool-rich place online for people who want to take the initiative to be a founder. To get a fuller picture of what it would look like to be a founder, go to www.hopefulneighborhood.org/founder and spend some time exploring the discover-imagine-pursue process, as well as the tools, aids, and coaching that the Hopeful Neighborhood Project has to offer. Then, reflect on what you've seen.

How does what you've seen affect your excitement or perceived barriers when it comes to being a founder?

Who are the neighbors you think would get most excited about being a part of this kind of process with you?

## SUMMARY

We spent this session discovering that a hopeful neighborhood is where neighbors create and work a plan together. But this won't just happen randomly; someone in the neighborhood needs to take the initiative. We have created a trustworthy process, simple tools, and a nationwide network for those who want to do just that. We invite you to take the first couple of steps in that process to see if you might be one of those people.

# Conclusion

## GIVING AND RECEIVING

*All of us, at some time or other, need help.*
*Whether we're giving or receiving help,*
*each one of us has something valuable*
*to bring to this world. That's one of the*
*things that connects us as neighbors—*
*in our own way, each one of us is a*
*giver and a receiver.*

**FRED ROGERS**

I f our culture has had a true champion of neighborhoods, it's
definitely Fred Rogers. His show, *Mr. Rogers' Neighborhood*, ran
for over thirty years and shaped how countless children and their
families thought about engaging with the people and place right
around them.

Rogers understood that "each of us has something valuable to
bring to this world." Consequently, this means that all of us need to
give and receive. It's important that we give to others from the gifts
we have. It's also important that we receive from others from the
gifts they have.

There is something kind and beautiful and human about this mu-
tuality. It is at once empowering (I have something valuable to offer)
and humbling (I need help from the people around me). Despite
what cartoons and movies may suggest, the world is not made up of
heroes who ride in to save the day and those in distress who are lying
there helpless.

We are all created to give and receive. To love and be loved. And that is what the Hopeful Neighborhood Project is all about. In fact, this is why the Hopeful Neighborhood Network exists: to connect founders and their groups with each other in a supportive, encouraging, mutual network.

The Hopeful Neighborhood Network is a place you can go to share your ideas and insights and encouragements. It's also a place you can go to learn from others. The network is a place for both giving and receiving. As you take the step to become a founder (gathering some neighbors together to pursue the common good of your neighborhood), consider joining this global network of other founders and groups.

The Hopeful Neighborhood Network is not only a place to give and receive valuable tips, ideas, and insights; it is also a place to give and receive invaluable encouragement, inspiration, and hope. We are both honored to be a part of this vibrant, growing network of neighbors—and we hope to meet you there.

# Acknowledgments

We are unapologetically standing on the shoulders of John L. McKnight and John P. Kretzmann and thank them and their colleagues at the Asset-Based Community Development Institute at DePaul University for their work in the area of community development. We are also indebted to Kristen Wagner, Claire Rippel, and all those involved in the Neighborhood Leadership Academy at the University of Missouri–St. Louis.

It would be difficult to overstate how essential the insights and hard work of Ashley Bayless and Jason Broge were in the writing of this Field Guide and the launching of the Hopeful Neighborhood Project. A deep *thank you* to you both.

# Notes

## SESSION ONE: FOCUS ON POSSIBILITIES

[1]Jake Meador, *In Search of the Common Good: Christian Fidelity in a Fractured World* (Downers Grove, IL: InterVarsity Press, 2019), 29.

## SESSION TWO: SHARE INDIVIDUAL GIFTS

[1]Tony Cook, "Preface," in *Better Together: How Christians Can Be a Welcome Influence in Their Neighborhoods* (Ventura, CA: Barna Group, 2020), 5.

## SESSION FOUR: LONG FOR NEIGHBORHOOD WELL-BEING

[1]Jay Bhatt, "Your Zip Code, Your Health," American Hospital Association, May 16, 2018, www.aha.org/news/insights-and-analysis/2018-05-16-your-zip-code-your-health.

## SESSION SIX: CREATE AND WORK A PLAN

[1]Barna Group, *Better Together: How Christians Can Be a Welcome Influence in Their Neighborhoods* (Ventura, CA: Barna Group, 2020), 48.
[2]Barna Group, *Better Together*, 59.

# Other Titles by Don Everts

*The Hopeful Neighborhood*
978-0-8308-4803-4

*The Reluctant Witness*
978-0-8308-4567-5

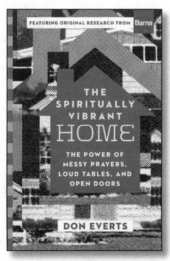

*The Spiritually Vibrant Home*
978-0-8308-4590-3

THE **HOPEFUL NEIGHBORHOOD PROJECT** ®

The Hopeful Neighborhood Project is a collaborative network committed to improving neighborhood well-being around the world. Our resources and online network equip and encourage neighbors to work together, using their gifts and the gifts of their community, to pursue the common good of their neighborhood.

*To find out more about our*
*active network and many resources visit us at*
**hopefulneighborhood.org.**